Full Circle:

A Life Taken So A Life Could Live
A Memoir

To Elaine

Thank You

Allison D. Williams

1/30/20

Allison D. Williams

Allison D. Williams

Full Circle

ISBN: 1-79150-459-0
ISBN-13: 9781791504595
10 9 8 7 6 5 4 3 2 1

CONTENTS

ACKNOWLEDGMENTS

First, I want to thank the creator of the heavens and the earth, for giving me life and the gift of articulation, and the confidence to speak out against injustice on any level. I would like to thank my mom's. My biological mom for giving me life and picking the most beautiful person on Earth to have me as her Only Daughter my mom and may she rest in peace, for loving me unconditionally and teaching me how to be a loving and nurturing human being, as she was, my best friend my everything. My Dad who gave me tough love who was the strictest but I look back and understood why he was. My six grade teacher Mr. D for giving me the longest writing assignment which enhanced my penmanship, which gave me a love for writing. Every person in my life that has ever encouraged and supported me, in my childhood, adolescence, all the way through my adulthood. Those experiences molded and shaped me into the woman I was destined to be. I thank the writing instructor of the class that I took right after my Son passed, although it wasn't therapy is was therapeutic in my healing. all the participants in this class that encouraged me to continue writing and telling my story. Thanking My Oldest Daughter that at the very beginning was my biggest fan she Attended the Harlem Renaissance and bought back business cards of authors for me to network with. Staying on me saying "Mom when are you gonna finish your book?". I believe everything happens for reason nothing is by chance, so I want to thank everyone who has been a positive force in my life, and in my Son's life. From family to friends to even complete strangers, whom I never knew would come up to me hug me and say they knew Elleek and loved him his smile his energy, thank you it got me through. We all need someone who's gonna love and encourage us to be all we can be even when we doubt ourselves. As the tears fall as they often do, just to get that text out of nowhere saying are you okay, is everything. I've been blessed to have someone to do just that. So to my Special Friend, thank you for being there. Lastly, I want to say before my Son passed he said Mom you should run for office or something you could make some changes. To my Son Elleek I may not be able to change the world from all the hate, poverty, mental illness, mental cruelty, domestic violence on all

levels. But I will always be a voice for you in the Political arena or on the Street Corner until I die. As well as be a Voice for those whose voice is crippled by pain. Elleek I truly believe your life served a great purpose, until we meet again I love you and miss you so much now and forever, without measure may you RIP and have no more worries. May God have Mercy on your Soul until we meet again you will

forever be in our hearts

CHAPTER ONE

I was brought to upstate New York when I was very young. I was very blessed and very fortunate to have the parents that I had. Growing up as an only Child was very lonely at times, especially because both my parents worked full time jobs. They had no handouts; no government assistance and they still provided it all. I looked up to them and had some sort of reference when it came to family. I was a very intelligent child. I was always the center of attention and knew how to speak and conduct myself. I was always curious and the curiosity got the best of me.

One day I started to notice small details about my parents and it made me see that I was a bit different from them. I remember thinking that our fingers and toes were different. That may seem minute but it was something I noticed. I was talking about it with a friend. You know as kids we talk, even though we don't know everything we are talking about. My friend blurted out "That's why you're adopted!"

I asked "What does that mean?" and their sister responded with a "Shh" telling her sibling to be quiet. I went home and said "Mommy, am I adopted?"

"Who said that?" she questioned and I told her that my friend was the one who did. My mom told me that wasn't true and to not listen to rumors. One day, while my Mother was at work someone called looking for her. The only thing was that my mom had a niece with the same name as her; I gave the phone to her, because the caller also had the same name as my mother's' niece. However, this was not a match but it was my Biological Mom trying to reach out to me, real spooky.

One day my Dad sat me down while my Mom was at work to have a talk to me. I was 12 years old at the time. He said that everything would be revealed in the silver box sitting on the table in front of me. He then stood up and said he would be right back. He didn't know how to tell me, so he positioned the paper to where I could read it. I saw who I was born as and it was different than the name given to me by who I thought were my real parents. I remember thinking that I was not who they said I was. I was in a state of shock when I found out I was adopted. I knew my Mother and Father loved me dearly and I never wanted for anything. However, finding out I came from somewhere else made me believe a part of my life was missing. I can't recall what it really was. I think I may have needed the love from my real parents and a sense of belonging from them.

So, as it pertains to love, I started looking for it in all the wrong places. Of course being an adolescent and having an identity crisis was challenging and even more so for my parents. This adoption situation gave me the right I thought to do what I wanted. I was a whole new me. I was mad at everyone for telling me at the time they did. I was especially angry at my parents. My hormones were raging and I was becoming a young woman. On top of not receiving anytime of counseling and the only response I received was "it's a good thing your mother gave you up because she couldn't take care of you."

I went through a period of extreme frustration, disappointment, hurt and shame. This went on for some time until I found out that my biological mother wanted to see me. I was told that I had siblings and it made me excited. It gave me hope because I was an only child. I wanted to see who my siblings were. I wanted to see my birth mother. Arrangements were made and my foreign family was set to come and see me.

It was a Saturday morning, right smack in the middle of summertime. There weren't many people up. But I was up asking my Mother a million questions. "Why does she want to see me? What should I say? What if she wants to take me?" All of the questions were tumbling from my mouth; one after the other. My mother said "no she just wants to see you; she hasn't seen you since you were a baby". I remember thinking that I didn't like that answer. I wanted my mom to want to see me because she made a mistake by giving me up, because she loved me and because her little girl was living in a world without her.

I was pacing back in forth to the window. "Oh! My God I think there here". I shouted. They pulled up in a gold beat down car. I watched from my spot as they got out of the car. I looked at the face of the woman who gave me up as she trotted alongside some guy. They knocked at the door and my aunt answered. She hugged my Mom and introduced her friend.

When she turned to face me my stomach dropped from the nervousness. "Hi Allison", she said. I replied back with a small "Hi". My mother instructed me to give her a hug so with a deep breath and small prayer, I did. She said that she tried to reach out many times before. However, she couldn't reach us because we moved. She was really kind and it made me open up a little. I showed her all of my awards I received as a track player. I had ribbons and metals. I started to shift uncomfortably again because she wouldn't stop staring at me. For some reason it made me want to curl up in a ball.

After a few more uncomfortable moments of silence she told me I had a brother and sister. She showed me a picture and I thought to myself that I looked like my sister so much we could've been twins. I smiled because I always prayed for a sister. In the photograph she was wearing a silver jacket and a white shirt with jeans. I thought she was very pretty and stylish. I couldn't wait to meet her. I was so excited and immediately asked my mom when I could go on a trip to meet her. I went to school on Monday and I brought my sisters' picture to show everyone. They all thought it was me but it wasn't.

CHAPTER TWO

I will never forget the day I got to meet my sister. This time my dad went with us to visit. They lived in the projects and when we pulled up my biological mother was standing outside waiting. We walked into the house and I impatiently asked where my sister was. The grown-ups started talking and I tried to stay calm. We finally made it upstairs to their apartment. It was fairly small; a cornered living area, petite kitchen and two bedrooms. When we sat down I kept whispering to my mom "where is my sister?" She asked my birth mother and she said that my sister ran out and that she would be back.

We stayed there a while. So long that it started to get dark and with the darkness my hope faded as well. I gave up on meeting her and wanted to go back home. As soon as I turned to tell my mom I was ready, my sister came running in. She stood right in front of me and it seemed like I was looking into a mirror... I froze.

My mom egged me on to stand up and hug her; reminding me that I couldn't stop talking about meeting her. So I did, I stood up and hugged my sister. It felt like a dream come true. She was on her way back out and I guess we both could feel that we didn't want to leave each other so soon. She saw my frown and asked my mom if I could go with her. I begged my mom and she told me to go ahead. Ecstatic, I followed my sister out the door. We got on the transit and I couldn't stop staring at her. She looked much older than me, but she was only a year older.

I asked where we were going and she said to her boyfriend's place. I thought to myself that I didn't have a boyfriend. Suddenly I had this aching need to have one. Her boyfriend looked like a grown man. We didn't stay long and headed back to her house a short while after. When we got back we started talking about our next trip to see each other.

I wanted to do everything that my sister did. I wanted to dress like her, talk like her, wear my hair like her and anything in between. The next time we met I told my mom that I wanted another outfit because it wasn't as nice as my sisters. My sister was wearing beads in her hair with plaits so I wanted them too. On that trip we talked about everything from boys, to clothes, to school and even sex.

On our next adventure, I met my biological dad. He lived in Wildwood, New Jersey, near the beach. Both of my moms' sat in chairs on the beach while my sister and I ran off to see our "Dad".

I was having fun, just being in a different place and being around a family I never knew I had. When we returned home, my Father was not too happy. He thought it was too much, too soon. I kind of thought he didn't want to lose me. He believed I would leave them to go and live with my biological parents. I assured them that even though I had grown to love my new family that it's not where I wanted to be.

Somehow during one of our visits my sister spoke about the possibility of her coming to live with me. All of the adults agreed to my surprise. I was very ecstatic to experience having a big sister around and she was able to see what it was like having a little brat for a sister.

I wanted to do everything big Sis did and we were way off when it came to a certain thing. She was much more mature than me and that's because she grew up having to do things at a faster pace. With her around I started to realize that I wanted a boyfriend, the stage for boys had set in.

***

I was a teenager and was just starting to see a boy for being cute. At first I never looked at a guy in that way. I was pretty cut off from the world of boys. It was in the late 70s; disco parties were in full effect. My sister was well on her way into this world and I felt as if I was behind. Our town was small; there wasn't much to do so I would walk the streets with my friends, looking for something to get into. My sister would never join me; it was a little too slow for her liking. Well, being regular and ordinary wasn't the groove; I needed some validation. I wanted popularity because I wasn't who everyone thought I was. They assumed I was like my sister but in truth I was behind. I wanted to be in the crowd.

Realizing that I wouldn't find the vibe I wanted in my hometown, I started to look elsewhere. One weekend I asked my mom if my sister and I could go over to my friend's house for the weekend. It was 30 minutes away from my normal life. My mom asked if there would be any parents home. I told her there would be and that my big sister wouldn't let anything happen to me.

Once we made to my friends I felt this sense of exciting freedom. There was great music, good vibes and cute boys; one cute boy in particular...

CHAPTER THREE

He was a popular Dj. We hit it off from the very beginning. For about 6 months we would talk on the phone for hours. Before long, I started to call him my "boyfriend". We exchanged gifts at Christmas, I met his parents and he met my mom. The puppy love was arising as so were the hormones. I decided I was ready for sex.

I was scared and nervous. I had never done it before and was scared to get in trouble. I was also afraid that it would hurt. I decided to go to my sister because she was older and more experienced. She would tell me the right thing. Honestly, I was looking for an excuse to put it off. I went next door to where my sister was. I asked her what I should do. I said "Sis I want to but I'm scared." I remember thinking that she would probably disapprove of me having sex. Although she was, she still considered me her innocent baby sister. In my mind I saw her hand smacking me across the face. I pictured her saying "No get you over here and stop being fresh." But instead she replied "Maybe you shouldn't then". After noticing the frown on my face she then asked "What do you want to do?"

That was the question of the day and I didn't know the answer. I only knew that I was tired of being the good girl. I wanted to be like all of the other girls, including my sister and experience being with a boy.

Well I did it and I was no longer the pure and innocent young girl. I had this picture in my mind that sex would bring us closer but it was nothing short of the exact opposite. We didn't get married and run into the sunset. Those were the thoughts of an inexperienced, naïve girl with no true guidance.

Although my fairy tale of having a perfect life with my guy didn't go as planned I still chose to lie down with him every chance I got. Thirty minutes away on the bus was far and sometimes if we were late, my sister and I would get a ride back home by his Dad. Losing my virginity changed me a little. I felt bolder and wanted to go against the grain more than I did before. I started to have small fights with my sister. I became territorial and call out everything that was mine. I would tell her "that is mine and you can go back home".

I guess I was feeling myself and it didn't make our relationship good. I had picked fights with her one time too many and it eventually sent her packing. I tried to apologize but it was too late. I count that as one of the biggest mistakes I ever made. I felt alone, when my Sister left, and my small town didn't make it any better.

I begged my mom to move. She did, realizing that it would be better for her job because she could be closer to it. We wouldn't have to catch the bus anymore. So, she found us a place. In the midst of all of this, somehow, my Dad became disconnected from our family. He wasn't supportive of the move we one weekend when he was out of town, we packed up and left. His focus wasn't on us and mom gave him enough time to change his mind. We were on our own.

Our fresh start was the summer of 1981. The city was a little bigger than the one we had left. We were closer to some of our other family and because of the constant visits I knew enough people to not be bored.

There was a piece of me that longed for my Dad to be with us. I admired the bike he bought me one year before and relished in the time we were all still a family. I knew he would be shocked when he arrived home to see that my mom had left him.

I was pleased with our new house, it was pink on the outside, the inside was very clean and cool. Some parts of it were paneled and it had a nice little backyard.

The house was decent but I was ready to hit the streets. I made a friend across town back when we were in our old place and it was time to let my wings spread. One day, I hopped on my bike to head there. My friend was surprised, she asked how I made it across town on my bike and I told her that we had moved closer to her. She was excited and had a bike too. I was happy that we could ride our bikes together and just be girls. Our rides led me into the arms of my next guy...

Chapter four

There was too much time on my hands and summer time was an excuse to use some of it, even if it would lead me down a bad path. I was on my way home when I saw someone that looked familiar. It wasn't him but it was his older brother. Upon a closer reflection I could tell they were different. I did not know exactly how old he was but I just thought to myself *age ain't nothing but a number.*

He seemed different, quieter. *Watch out for the quiet ones.* At first nothing seemed to be off or wrong about him. His brother told me he didn't have a girlfriend and that was all I needed to hear at the time. I was vulnerable; my mom and dad were separated and my mom wasn't hard on me like my dad was. I used this to my advantage; sadly I considered my mom to be carefree and a real pushover.

One summer night we met up and he ended up walking me home. I am not sure exactly what he said at first but I just remember him making me feel like it was safe to be around him and that he could be trusted. Of course, he knew how naïve and vulnerable I was. We made it to my house and he said "I don't want come in; I just want to make sure you're safe". I believed him and was in awe of his kindness. I only thought about him wanting me to be safe.

It was a windy evening. Once we arrived to my house I volunteered to walk him back to the corner. As we walked, he held me tightly. He was much older and put me in remembrance of my dad but I couldn't separate the two. As he started to loosen his hold on me I started crying after holding on to him even tighter. I didn't know anything about loving a man.

The only man I knew about loving was my Dad and I was burdened with the fact that my mom left him. I started to think of this guy as the next best thing. He asked me what was wrong and I told him nothing, "I just don't want you to leave". I started to feel attached and it was deeper than I realized. Although I was the one who approached him I knew this was bad. He was seven years older than me. I was way too young for him and he could go to jail. That was considered statutory rape. Nothing happened that night, he just left after walking me back to my door.

My mom worked 11 to 9 everyday so I had a lot of freedom to move around, more than I should have. I had a brother but he wasn't a part of my life. I had no real male figures. My dad still hadn't made an appearance to fight for his family and I remember thinking that he was probably just still in shock and upset.

Once we exchanged numbers and started hanging out, the age thing didn't stop anything. It came up but we went along and just kept it a secret. I had my second boyfriend. Things with my friends started to change because we did everything together. We rode our bikes, took pictures at the park, and wore the same t shirts and all the stuff new couples do. People would see us walking and he knew lots of people. They were always speaking and I felt like a prized possession. This was the type of popularity I thought I wanted.

I had no one to tell me the dos and don'ts. I wasn't on any birth control because during that time the elders believed that *no sex was safe sex*. I soon realized that I was in too deep. We were at his house and I went downstairs to call my mom. That is when I heard someone on the other line saying "tell me you love me". I was in pure shock and slowly hung up the phone. He came downstairs and the look on my face must've alerted him.

***

I saw something flash behind his eyes. There was something raw and untamed lying there. He said "let's go!" It was a uncensored demand and I became scared. He was walking ahead of me and as I stood in the back I remember thinking that something was wrong with him. I prayed to have my dad or brother around or someone who could protect me. As we were walking, his brother says to go in another yard. My guy, the guy I loved and only saw goodness in turned to me and screamed "why are you listening to other people?!"

Before I could even understand the question he smacks me. My mind was in a haze. I told him that I wouldn't listen to anyone but to just not him me again. Then I started to apologize as if I did something wrong. He told me that I was the reason for his behavior. He brother looked and remained silent. He didn't speak or try to help me.

I knew I had gotten myself into a big mess. I think his brother assumed I was older and that I didn't need or want to be saved. He had no idea that I was only fifteen. I thought what my guy showed me was his version of love. It may sound crazy but it is what I believed. That was the excuse that appeared after the hurt I felt and the disappointment that this man wasn't who I thought he was. *Is this love? Maybe he really loves me already.*

My friends started to come back around wanting me to talk to them and hang out but I was scared. My guy knew where I lived and who I lived with. Afraid that I would reveal what he did to me I chose to say nothing to my friends. I didn't say a word to anyone. I continued the relationship as if nothing ever happened.

We were wearing our matching tees one day while riding our bikes. He always rode in front of me. Some random guy spoke to me. Maybe he was too nice or maybe he was flirting. My guy definitely thought it was the latter because he threatened the stranger for saying something to me. I thought to myself, *this is dangerously insane...*

Chapter Five

Regardless of how I felt about my guys actions I went on like normal. He started staying over sometimes when it got late and ended up spending the nights with me. I was at school and one day he showed up, waiting outside for me. I wasn't expecting so see him so it took me by surprise, at that point everything did.

One of my friends shouted "isn't that your boyfriend outside?" Panicked I blurted out "Where, Omg, it is", once I looked down and saw him. I didn't know what to do and didn't want to go outside. It didn't matter that we spent most of our nights together. I felt trapped and honestly my days at school gave me time to be away from him. I started to think that love shouldn't feel this uneasy.

Once I got outside I tried to appear to be in shock, the good kind of shock but I knew fear was all over my face. The last thing I wanted him to see was fear. My teenage life was over before it began. My friends told me that it wasn't love. After I finally revealed him hitting me they told me to leave and leave him alone. *I couldn't.*

Chapter six

My father finally paid us a visit, I thought to myself *better late than ever*. He asked me if I knew my guy and I denied it. My father revealed that he heard I knew and that he also knew my guys mother. I don't know how but somehow my dad got wind of what was going on. He told me "when you do see him, tell him I'm looking for him." The words may have been simple but I saw the anger behind my father's eyes.

I told my guy but still continued seeing him. At that point, I was protecting him from everyone even though the relationship was toxic. I didn't want any harm to come to him, regardless of the harm he caused me. He said he saw my dad out one night while he was at a bar. He dipped down behind the bar, in shock. He had never seen my dad except for in the pictures my mom still kept of us on our floor model television.

From that day forward he dodged my dad and I helped him. Later that summer I found out that I was pregnant. Fear and shame came over me once I knew I had to tell my mom. It was the hardest thing I ever had to do. She asked me what I was going to do. I didn't have the answers, of course I didn't. I was still waiting on someone to come save and protect me from what I'd gotten myself into. She wanted to know how I would take care of a child, a teenager still in school with a baby's father who didn't have a job or any time of future planned.

I wanted to get rid of it and told him I didn't think we should go through with having a child. *Why did I say that?* He threatened to get a bus ticket and leave. At that time, that thought of him leaving me was worse than us having a baby together. Oh god, I thought, *okay I guess we're having a baby.*

His mother didn't allow the type of activity we had going on. Unlike my mother who was not there for me in the way that I needed, his didn't want any girls hanging around her house. Instead of going on with him I should've listened to her and stayed away. Low and behold I stayed in school and carried my son.

After high school I went to the pilot program. It was alternative schooling for teen moms. There were two classrooms that encompassed all of our subjects. We had good food, good mentors and a tight little community. We all went into labor one by one.

I didn't have any real issues during my pregnancy. My Dad visited again and after learning I had chosen to keep the baby he told me he wanted nothing to do with me. I guess his heart was broken, because he wanted so much more for me.

My mom was out one day and my guy came over. A little before he got ready to leave out I felt my stomach cramping, I said "I think it's time".

It was unlike anything I had felt the entire nine months. Once we made it to the hospital they told me that my water didn't break but that I had to stay because I was going into labor. My guy left, saying he'd be back and I was officially admitted. The following 24 hours was extremely hard. The doctors had to use forceps because I couldn't push my baby out. At sixteen years old I gave birth to a healthy baby boy on May 15, 1982. He was 8ibs and 7 ounces.

His father was the happiest man on earth and I thought that maybe he'd treat me like a queen since I brought forth life and gave him a son. He ran through the hospital doors and around the park in his surgical suit, announcing that his son was born.

I just wanted rest; I didn't have much time to process anything. But before long, I had to start thinking about being a mom. Mine came to visit me but we really didn't talk much. We both pretty much ignored the elephant in the room about my baby's father being older, before and after the birth. She asked me if he'd signed the birth certificate and I told her he hadn't.

We spent so much time just looking at our baby. Both of our families were in and out and to my surprise my Dad made an appearance. As he walked in holding a teddy bear, I said to myself *I thought you didn't want anything to do with me.* He kept his word; he didn't want anything to do with me. It was all about my son, Elleek.

As I was holding him my dad told me that he wasn't there for me. I just smiled, although torn up on the inside. I thought to myself that I would make sure my son would be loved, unconditionally. He didn't deserve anything less.

My dad told me "I'm here for him; you get nothing from me, no more". Deep down I knew he still loved me and was just still hurt. He just wanted so much more for me and so much more for me to do with my life. At the time, he couldn't see that my story wasn't over. I remember thinking that he wasn't short of imperfections either. There was a reason my mom left him but I guess he forgot the role he played in that. I told him it was fine. He kissed me and walked out.

My baby's father is the one to choose the name. It was a combination of his middle name, his sister's middle name and his nephew's. We were admiring our son when I noticed a picture he'd brought with him. It was taken with a female and it seemed to be up close and personal. I questioned him and he got defensive. Maybe I pushed the wrong button because he left and never returned. His name never made it on the birth certificate.

CHAPTER SEVEN

I couldn't worry about him anymore. Something in me changed and I was only concerned about the little life I'd just given birth to. I wanted to focus on my beautiful baby boy. Being a teenage mom I didn't know anything about the responsibilities that came with caring for another life. I just knew I couldn't give up. My mom was by my side though and I knew I would have to learn.

I decided to breastfeed after learning the expenses of milk. I found out how to care for my son from my aunts and mom. There were small things like how to wash his fact to avoid infections. It was the small things that I wouldn't have known without their help.

After one week I took my newborn to see his other grandmother. I had a new respect for her because she was also a teen mom at one point and had cared for her many children. She showed me how to mold and shape my sons head so it wouldn't have what she called a *cone shaped head*. She taught me how to keep his skin smooth by using a wet diaper to wash his face. I thought that was odd but still went along with it.

He looked just like his Dad as a babe and her face lit up as she held him. I am sure she pictured her son when she did. The breastfeeding was a challenge.

One weekend my cousin begged me to go out. I saw no problem with getting some air for a couple of hours. I thought I would feed him and that he would be good. Within two hours of me being out, my breast started to leak. I tried to hide it because I didn't want to ruin everyone's night. But once my cousin took notice she said it was time for me to go. When I got there my mom had already given him a bottle of formula with some Enfamil and kayro syrup. I was not happy but I refused to question the woman who raised me.

My son's father had left for a period of time, out of town, to God knows where. I assumed it was to visit a female. Well he got stranded and I had to pay to get him home. Once he got there he noticed two of my friends were over, a male and a female. He called me into the room and asked me who they were, I told him and he started hitting me. I was the mother of his child. That didn't stop him. I was still sore after giving birth and that didn't stop him either. He called the boy into the hallway to *question him*. Next thing I knew to never come back after rustling with him. Some things never change, I thought. Mindless of the fact that he hadn't changed, I still let him back in. One morning we woke up and he was yelling at me around our son. My mother came out and told him to leave.

He was angry but still grabbed his bag and put it in the hallway. Then he went into the kitchen and the next thing I knew I heard the silverware drawer open so I ran out of the house because I knew his anger was directed towards me.

I started to run up the stairs to a neighbors and I noticed he was on my heels. The lady immediately opened the door letting me in. He went around back and started throwing rocks at the window. That's what my son would be exposed to. I knew that would be the behavior he would witness when he grew up.

I didn't want my son to be affected. I knew I had to get out of that situation and make sure I didn't have any more children by him. I just felt so overwhelmed and violate because my mom and I were alone. My father didn't visit regularly and there were still no male figures in our life. There was no one to protect us.

I tried to move on in the hopes he wouldn't come back. It was time for me to try to live as a teenager, outside of being a new mother. I was out at the skating rink when I was called to the front desk. His sister had to let me know that he'd been arrested. It was very bitter sweet.

I started to enjoy my freedom and try to live with less fear of being beaten. Going out became a privilege. I didn't have much to worry about though because my son was always in good hands. We were out again when I told a guy that I had a son. Next thing you know we were getting to know one another.

I didn't feel like I was cheating because I told him who my son's father was. It didn't seem to matter; eventually they sentenced my son father. He was away for a little while and reality started to set that this would be the norm for us. I needed more, wanted some stability for my son. I wanted someone who could provide for us. That is what I saw growing up.

I later did what I said I would never do. I took my son inside the jailhouse so his father could see him. I wish I vowed to be done with him. I was sick of the abuse, I didn't deserve it and neither did my son.

I knew I had been looking for love in all the wrong places and I just wanted to move forward.

This new guy had a little more to offer me. It may have not been the best thing to do but it was keeping me and my son safe. This guy had the intention to make my life better even after he knew my situation. At first, I was ready to deal with the consequences however they came. I thought that maybe the time away would make my baby's father finally to the right thing by us. So in my heart I held out hope that he would come out of jail a better man than he went in.

My new relationship was a lot better but I still insanely held out hope for the previous one. I was busy doing something one day while a friend was visiting and my new guy answered my phone after hearing it ring. I overheard him telling my baby's father to not call anymore. I was frustrated and asked why he did it; I told him it wasn't his place. I was living in the present but my past still had some type of hold on me. I think I was more afraid that anything. I didn't want any bad blood because I knew what my ex was capable of. Once he was out it would be a problem. My new guy didn't care. I think he was trying to prove a point.

My ex had already called me previously and said he heard I was seeing someone. I was concerned because he was set to come home a few days later. I had two options. I could stick out in my new relationship and except that things had gotten better for me, or I could run back to my ex after he came home.

I, of course took the latter. I told my new guy that my son's father was coming home and that whatever we had was over. I told him I had to stay with him for the sake of our son. In reality, it was more about fear.

CHAPTER EIGHT

He came home around midnight. The moon had a dimming glow and so did his mood. I could tell he was bothered by the situation but he acted nonchalant. That made me more uneasy because I was waiting on the other shoe to drop. Deep down I prayed that his jail time changed him and that we could move past our negative history.

My gut started to twist and turn and I could feel the contents of my stomach threatening to come out. I was washing the dishes while he sat in a chair behind me. Maybe the entire time contemplated what was going on while he was locked up. He probably thought how *dare I talk to anyone?*

Being locked up didn't teach him anything. The next thing I saw was his foot coming at me. He started kicking me in my shins, damn! That hurt but I held it in and asked why he was kicking me. Then, there was a ring at the door. I'm thinking *oh my God I told this dude not to come here so I hope it's not him.* I walked to the door, filled with trepidation...

It was *him*. I peeked out the door and whispered for him not to come back anymore because my baby's father was back. I'd already told him it was over so it boggled me that he would reappear at my doorstep. On my trip back into the house I heard the question. *Who was that?*

I didn't want to answer. My words were trapped in my throat. Paused in my spot he started to shake his head as if he already knew the answer. I was still in the same spot as I glanced at him walking to the door. My feet automatically started moving behind him, quietly and I watched as he stuck his arm out and waved for my recent ex to come back. My entire body started to shake. I had no idea what he would do. I was so scared that I rushed to close the door, locked it and ran to the window. When he got close enough my sons father opened the door and hit him, they started fighting.

I could hear my mother's voice telling *me to leave both of their asses alone.* I just knew *he* wanted to get at me.

After some rustling the guy took off in his car. My son's father leaves too. I told my mom that I had to get Elleek and leave because it wasn't safe for us there. I called a friend who was near and town, asking her to have her boyfriend come and get me and my son. In the midst of it the ding comes again. I opened the door in a panic right after I notice blood spilled on the floor. To my surprise it was a police officer.

I didn't know how but they said they'd found a man bleeding in the park and that he was brought to the hospital. It was my son's father. The man in uniform wanted to know who he'd been fighting with and how to find them. I was a witness to what had happened. I'm thinking to myself *how the hell did I get myself into this?*

I reluctantly gave up my new found friends identity because my son's father was injured and even though he deserved it, I was more afraid of what he'd do to me if I didn't help the police find his abuser.

While I was waiting, the phone rang, "hello",

It was his aunt, she said, "listen bitch you called the police on my nephew, bring all the shit he bought you back, if my nephew goes to jail you're gonna get your ass beat".

Little did she know, I begged; even warned him not to come back there. I got in touch with him and told him to just stay away. I felt bad because I knew he just cared for me and hated that I went back with my son's father. I just wanted it all to be over so I told him that the cops were looking and to just lay low.

My ride came and I took my son to safety, telling my mom I'd call her once I made it to my destination. My baby was only five months all. I knew that he could feel all my energy and pain. In his little mind he probably wondered what was going on.

I never wanted to raise my child in a negative or dysfunctional environment. I just felt trapped. I didn't know how to break away from his father without the fear of what he'd do if I left him for good.

My friend was much than me. She told me that I better be careful and if he did those things around my baby then he'd do anything. She told me that if I continued to raise my son around him that once he got older he would take on the same traits as his father. I sure as hell didn't; want my son to disrespect a woman and I damn sure didn't want him physical or mentally abusing one.

I didn't really think much of what she was saying. I knew if to be true but I was just grateful to be out of town and away from everything. His father couldn't find us. He had no idea where we were and he didn't have a vehicle…

Chapter Nine

After I settled in for a bit and calmed down, I asked my friend if she could watch Elleek while I went to the store. I had already asked my recent ex to stay away after the ordeal with the police at my house but he obviously didn't care. As I was walking to the store, low and behold, he pulls up. *Are you kidding me?*

I asked him what he was doing way over there and how did he even know where I was. He said he wasn't mad and that he just wanted to talk.

I said "you're the reason why I'm in this mess, I told you not to come around".

I told him that everyone wanted to do something to me. His family was threatening me, although I did nothing wrong. He said that no one would lay a finger on me. Regardless of what had happened, I trusted him. I knew he wouldn't put his hands on me or harm me. His anger was directly towards Elleeks father.

I contemplated for a bit and then said "well you have to take me to see my son's father". I knew it wasn't my fault but I still felt bad for him being beaten. My intention was to stay away but I was still weak. He said we could go and that he would apologize for everything.

So, I gathered my Son, thanked my friends and went back home. They wished me luck and said to call once I made it back. I could read the looks on their faces... *you're stupid. Why would you go back there?* And the many other thoughts that I'm sure were rolling through their minds. Once I made it home, I took a shower and got dressed. Elleek stayed with my mother and we headed to the hospital.

When we arrived there was a girl there that he had been with before, some girl that didn't care that we had a son, some girl who was either oblivious or accepting of his irrational behavior.

At any rate, I wanted to see how he was and my new ex wanted to apologize. He did. They both acknowledged they were wrong, shook hands and called it even. I thought it was funny how Elleeks father could apologize to a man but never once did so to me for all of the many things he'd done.

I left him where was; his mouth wired shut shortly after the exchange from the beating he'd taken. I just wanted to be left alone and was grateful to go back to my son, even though I was exhausted.

I took my little babe in my arms and looked into his eyes. "This is not the life I wanted for you, I promise things are not gonna stay like this." I watched his innocent face as the tears I'd held back for so long trailed down mine; with the hope I could stand by my word.

The next day I went to the hospital by myself because I felt so bad. He was getting ready to be discharged. I looked over and saw the same girl was there again. I had had enough. Clearly it was over between the two of us. I looked at him and said "I'm leaving".

I heard the "No you're not" reply as I turned to head back out the room. The order stopped me in my tracks.

The nurse came in with the discharge papers and I watched as his voice became louder. I guess my comment ticked him off. *Why did I come here?* I thought to myself. Well, I had and we ended up leaving the hospital together. The three of us…

CHAPTER TEN

On our way to the house he started hitting me. The girl just sat, watching. A few times she asked him to stop and a few other times she thought it was funny. After some threats he had the nerve to walk me home. This was probably so he could make sure I was there; in case he wanted to come back and finish the job. What a coward!

There were more times after that. More times where I took black eyes, threats on my life and anything else he threw at me. There was so much going on with the abuse, that I couldn't even be a good Mother to my Son.

The next time; he went to get a knife. I just knew he would kill us all. At that point it was very clear what I had to do. I had to leave his ass alone. That's what I did, I clung to the only help I knew and the only person that was going to protect me. Love had nothing to do with it.

It was about survival and I did what I had to do. My son was six months old. I never planned on having another man raising him but I had to live. gonna get a knife, and kill us all. At this point it was very clear what I had to do. Leave his ass alone!

As far as I was concerned my son couldn't miss what he never had anyway. His father was never in his life. The guy wasn't really about my son either; he was about me and protecting me but at that point it was enough. I would still be able to provide my son with a two parent household.

I became involved with this guy; he sold drugs, used them and eventually introduced me to them as well. That landed him in the penitentiary but when he came home he had a new perspective. He wanted to live a different way and if I wanted to be with him I would have to jump on board. The first thing he said was that I'd have to be okay with him having more than one woman. It was the way of life for those who followed Islam, his newfound religion. Hell no! I did not want to deal with that!

My first thought was that if I left him I would probably end up back with my son's father. I would have to get used to being abused and possibly having more children. I didn't want that either. I had to weigh my options and they were slim to none. Outside of my mom and her family, telling me "no more babies", there were no programs for teen pregnancy and awareness.

That was the situation I am sure many girls my age dealt with or worst. You know the thought. *If he could change his life and settle down, then I could be with him.*

At the end of the day, I figured I didn't have anything to lose. I converted to the Islamic Faith and we eventually got married. My mom felt that I was good to go as long as there were no drugs involved. My dad gave his blessing or should I say approval. He wanted what all dads want for their daughter; someone to take care of her as he would, respect her and treat her with kindness.

My life changed from then on in terms of freedom and religion. I was raised in a diverse religious background. My mother was Baptist and attending church moderate to occasional. She believed that you could get the same benefit staying home as you would going to the sanctuary. She said that churches were full up hypocrites. My dad on the other hand, was a free spirit. He went to a different church every Sunday.

I was just happy my son was in a better environment, even though my life had turned many times over. He was loved and taken care of. My parents provided anything. I didn't have to do too much other than provide love and guidance. Elleek was the only child for seven years. I became more responsible as a mother when I married and moved out of my mom's house. I embraced the new religion and way of life. Once I accepted Islam I wanted to forget all that happened before. It was a clean slate and I wanted nothing more to do with my old life. I became a part of a new community that welcomed and embraced me with open arms. I was ready to submit and do everything the Creator expected from me. Unfortunately, that wasn't the case for the person I decided to that that with.

My husband found that one thing that allowed him to be who he truly was. He was able to have more than one woman. He stopped at nothing to have it all. It was never about building and reforming himself to improve the mental or physical well-being of his family. It was about being in control and having everything his way. I knew I couldn't change him. So I settled. I owed that to my son. I wanted him to benefit the most.

Elleek became my priority. I made sure he had food, clothing and a home. It was new for me since I got my start late after living at home for so long. He had his own room. I took pride in cooking for him and everything else a mom does for her child. Before long that would expand since I was pregnant with my second child.

Chapter Eleven

There was a strain on me and the pregnancy due to the fact that I nearly lost my child. My husband was a manipulator at heart. I was in an emotional roller coaster and it took a toll on my body. You can take the person out the streets but you can't take the streets out the person. I found out he was trying to convert a woman from his past. On a cold winter night, two women came to my house looking for someone who didn't live there. I could tell they were lying and didn't expect to see me answering the door. Shortly after he left out, I followed him. His expression dropped when he saw my car. He came outside immediately. I knew our marriage wasn't right; however that was part of the religious rights he had as a "man". My insides flipped over and over from the hurt I felt. There I was, pregnant again; wanting to be a happy mother with child but it didn't go that way.

I drove around the park shivering; even from the inside of my car the cold crept in through the cracks. Maybe I was only half way there because on my way home I slid on the ice and almost hit a tree. When we got home I felt my stomach cramping up and soon after there was some spotting but it vanished shortly after.

On July 18, 1988, I gave birth to another beautiful healthy baby boy. Elleek was a big brother, at the age of seven and he was so happy. Regardless of what went on with the adults, in his eyes I was creating a family; for him. But he didn't understand everything going on. My husband demanded Elleek call him "uncle" based on the religion. He also said that he would only provide the food and shelter for him; that it wasn't his responsibility to provide his clothes and other necessities. I thought that was rude but I went along with it because my parents provided anything he slacked. I wanted him to have a relationship with his father, outside of what he and I went through. However, being a father was an impossible task for my ex. His stipulation required us to be together and the consequence for me not abiding was him not being involved in Elleeks life. I accepted my fate and went on; like I always did.

My husband and I had a joyful baby. There was love all around from both my parents and his father's mother. Elleek was just thrown in the loop. At the time, he was too busy playing and being a little boy to notice what was around him. It wasn't until after I started having more children that he could tell a difference being made towards him; not by me but by his "protector". Once the he was old enough to realize that his siblings coined the term "Dad" while he was stuck with "Uncle", there were questions. Nevertheless, he still didn't want for anything. But I figured in his mind he pondered why isn't my father around?.

Chapter Twelve

Several Years later...

Elleek had grown into a young man and it still awed me. As a mother, your child never really grows up in your eyes but he had and my heart leaped at the thought. He was the oldest of my nine children. Our life had taken us in different directions but I still loved him with everything in me.

One day, after finding out where he was staying I told him I had some mail for him. At that time he was enrolled in a local college so I figured the mail was rather important. We were both enrolled there but didn't see each other much. His advisor informed me that he hadn't attended his classes and wanted me to check on him to find out the issue. I was very concerned and dropped everything to locate him. Regardless, of what happened he was still my priority. In the end all he had was me.

He always wanted to do well and make me proud and because of that I stayed in his corner. What Mother wouldn't? My mom was also one of his biggest supporters so I always kept her in the loop whether the situation was good or bad. He was using her address as his legal residence and she wanted to go with me to find him.

Once we arrived at the place where he lived, I went straight to the door and rang the doorbell. A unfamiliar young girl answered and said he would be right out. I wondered who she was. There were so many things I didn't know about Elleeks life. I prayed to the heavens that he was there because he didn't have a vehicle. I always prayed for his safety being that he traveled by foot.

I saw him peek out from the basement of the apartment before he came to the car. He was wearing a white tee, a pair of worn blue jeans and two bare feet. The sun baked his skin as he ran to us. He spoke to his Grandmother first before acknowledging me.

"Hi Son", I said "What's going on? Your advisor said you haven't been to class, is everything okay?" I couldn't really sit still. My mother instincts made me nervous and anxious. I hoped he wasn't in some kind of trouble. Before he even spoke, I saw the pain and fear in his eyes. It made me sick to my stomach. I wished I could wipe that away from him with just a touch from my fingers.

"I can't do this" he shouted

"Why? What do you mean?"

"Mom, you don't understand people are shooting at me!!"

It seemed as if parts of my soul started to leave my body. In a haze I heard myself say "What?!"

"Somebody was shooting at me the other day" he replied

I didn't want to believe what he was telling me. Some part deep down wanted to forget that he'd ever said those words to me.

"That's your past son, you are going to school now and you're working on getting better, everything will be good soon" I told him

He stared at me as if I had two heads.

"It doesn't matter Ma, I have to look over my shoulder everywhere I go"

I had never seen him so hurt, scared and angry. I knew he didn't want to live like that. I could see the fear in his eyes and in his voice. I told him to come back home with me or to his Grandma's house. I wanted him to be as far away from the hood as possible, it wasn't safe.

His response was "No, I'm just a dead man walking!"

My mother was sitting across from me. I know she shared my trepidation. "Elleek it's gonna be okay" I heard her say.

"We have to go now" she said. I told her to hold on and made sure he would be at that location for us to reach him. He stumbled away, broken.

On the drive back, my mom pointed out that what she saw in his eyes wasn't good. We were both so worried about him. She said he was probably on drugs or something and I combatted it. "No Mom, he's just really worried about being shot at" I said, in defeat.

Chapter Thirteen

I prayed for my first born before that day but I prayed even harder after. I had no choice but to let him live his life. I couldn't force him out of the hood and I couldn't make him safe. The summer went on.

On Elleeks end he was making a store run with his cousin. He got out and his cousin stayed in the car. As he was coming out of the store, a familiar car pulled up. They directed him to come close to the car. He told them no and went to turn in the opposite direction. That landed him a bullet wound to his upper thigh.

His cousin took him to the hospital. The phone call revealing he'd been shot and taken to the hospital took the breath away from my body.

I rushed there, to find my son sitting up on the edge of the bed. Relieved that he was was alive, I only had time to glance at the two strange girls sitting in the room. I made sure he was okay and he revealed that he was but that the bullet would have to stay in his leg.

He told me that he knew the person who shot him but when I asked he refused to answer. I knew he was scared. I could also tell that he was becoming immune to the things happening to him and around him; that was my biggest fear. My mind went in overdrive. Was that resilience? Did he feel invincible?

I begged him to tell me. He refused to give me a name but he did give me a reminder of an event we both attended previously. He told me that the person who shot him was at the event.

"So are you going to tell the police?" I ask

He responded with a sunken "No!".

"Why Not?!" I scream "He's gonna be out here so he can do it again?!"

"Ma, leave, just go!"

Those words cut me deeper than his bullet wound. I was his Mother and first and foremost I didn't care about no code of the streets. But he didn't want to hear that. He couldn't comprehend it.

So, I went outside to gather my thoughts. Shortly after, one of the girls came out to comfort me from his rude and disrespectful outburst. She was his girlfriend's sister.

"Don't mind him, he's just scared but he loves you" I heard her say through the clutter in my mind.

She told me that Elleek talked about me all the time. In turn, I revealed that I was afraid of losing my son to the unsafe streets. I didn't know what to do.

My feet followed alongside hers, or maybe behind as we trotted back to his room. I figured it could only get worse from there. His mind was made up and as his mother, I couldn't fix it for him. I had to let him be a man and live his own life. The Doctors discharged him and I was able to take them home. They had decided to move to a different location. It was another basement apartment but my son was safe. Deep in my belly though, I was so afraid I would lose him to the streets. He slipped passed me on crutches and I told him that I loved him. I was just grateful to God for sparing his life.

After he settled in for a bit, I checked up and tried to help in any way I could. The next day he called me and I asked how he was doing. He told me he was gonna be laid up for a while so I went out to pick up some groceries. It still scared me that the person was still out there because he refused to reveal the guy. My cart filled with things for him but my mind kept going back to the same thought. Maybe they won't be done until he's dead...

Chapter Fourteen

Over the years I had become a very light sleeper. When you have children who are at the age where they roam you tend to sleep with one eye open. I had teenagers and they came in the house at all hours of the night.

May 16, 2006

It was a long, hard day of work. After my shift, I made sure my kids and house were taken care of. I finally fell asleep after I shower and quick wash to my scrubs. The ring struck an irritated nerve in me by its loud rattling. I checked the time and it noted 12:30 a.m.

There was no preparation but I leapt out of bad anyhow and with no hesitation I lifted the phone to my ear. On the other end, was yelling and screaming. The words "Your son has been shot" echoed somewhere deep within.

Why? Within the same year was I having to go through that again? I thought.

I wondered how many chances he would have after just being shot just four months prior. Only that time he survived with minor injuries. My maternal instincts tried to rear its head but I pushed the thoughts back down.

Somewhere unknown. God knows I couldn't handle it if something serious happened to my son. I thought.

I knew he it had to be a time where he would get one more chance at survival.

The phone fell out of my hands with an almost silent drop. I was ready to run out and jump in the car to go get my son but I heard my kids father say "No I'm taking you".

The ride on the highway was bumpy and uncertain. I couldn't process time properly but I know the drive to the hospital seemed like hours instead of half an hour. I yelled out for the car to move faster. Inside I prayed for God to let nothing happen my son. Please let him live.

I was ready to spend hour after nursing him back to health. I couldn't let my mind wander to the worst case scenario. Over and over. The one thought kept rewinding and replaying itself. I was in the middle of a continuing script. What did I do wrong? What could I have done to prevent this from happening?

Did I not love him enough? Did my protection fall short? Maybe I didn't do everything I could do. We finally get off the thruway and make it to the city driving area where everything took place. Time moved in slow motion. I wanted to get to my first born.

My legs carried me through the hospital and down the emergency room hall. I was afraid to keep moving. With each step, I wanted to take another one backwards. But I had to go and see what was wrong with my son.

I silently accused every person who looked my way. There was a room full of people, sitting, staring at me. They were there and I wasn't but yet they did nothing! I didn't want to face it.

I couldn't have people telling me that my son wasn't gonna make it. He had to make it!

I had to bring him home. I saw myself in front of the triage and let them know that my son was brought in. "We are doing everything we can, give us a minute please" I heard the young lady say.

"No!, I want to see my son right now!" I said it in my head before the words came spilling loudly from my mouth. Whatever was going on, he needed to know that I was there. The nurse explained that they couldn't accommodate me going back and all I saw was red flashing before my eyes. I blacked out. I was still there but I wasn't.

I came up with all sorts of scenarios to get me in the back. Maybe I could tell them I had a headache and they would send me back to get treated. My thoughts were lost when another nurse came back out. She nodded to me to come and I followed behind dreadfully. Inside the room she explained to me what was going on. My son had been shot three times.

She assured me that they would update me when they could. My hands were jittery. It was the nervousness taking over my entire being. I knew I needed some support. Instead of making phone calls to the wrong people I called one of my daughters. She went to be comforted by her friends and I sat feeling alone, even though their father was there with me.

The anger and resentment towards him came over me like a bolt of lightning. I truly believed my son would not have fought so hard had he been more of a father figure for him. But I knew it wasn't the time nor place. I called my Mother, regrettably. I didn't want to tell her what had happened. It hurt me to tell her that the boy she had raised was probably fighting for his life.

I paced back and forth, trying to be patient. Shortly after I was informed that they were moving him into surgery. I thought about my sons living situation. He was living on his own and involved in a lot of stuff in the streets. I believed it was because of the things that were going on at home. I contemplated on how many times my son needed me but my husband prevented me from seeing him. I told him before that if anything ever happened to Elleek that I would resent him for it. And there I was, lying in a pile of indication.

The detective showed up to question me and let me know that they were going to find out what happened and would be working on the case. It became more and more apparent that it was a homicide. I just wanted my son to pull through and honestly I wished death on the person who did that to him. Everyone started to file into the larger waiting area where the surgery took place. People came in and out, somewhat oblivious to me. The doctor walked in and I was ready to hear anything other than my son made it through. My legs pulled me closer to him with my husband, other sons and uncles walking behind me. The unpleasant look on his face told me the answer before I ever spoke the words. "How is my son?"

I never heard what he said in response. My ears filled up with invisible water and the world around me disappeared. "I'm sorry, we did all we could do" his words faded along with my body as I dropped to the floor. I wanted to run and get my son. I wanted to tell them that they had the wrong person and made a mistake.

Around 3:30 a.m. I stood over my first born lifeless body, identifying the face I'd loved for twenty something years. I couldn't accept the fact that he was not going to get up. The warmth of his cooling body stayed in my skin like a tattoo I'd just had done.

My family walked me out to the lobby where everyone else was. Once I walked in everyone just stared. Upon their faces lay sadness and from their lips was silence. No one spoke.

Again, in my head, I accused everyone for doing nothing to save my son. Why were they even there?

The revolving doors pierced my skin and I realized I didn't want to walk through them. I stopped. I wanted to go back inside because I couldn't grasp that that was my final goodbye or that I was leaving without my son. I was then escorted to the car. After a short argument with my husband, I realized that I was not in control of what was happening around me. So I got in the car, taking his advice that I needed some rest. I just didn't have the strength to keep fighting. The ride home was fairly mute. We pulled into the driveway and I felt as if the weight of the world was on my shoulders.

I didn't know how to tell the rest of my children that their brother was dead. I didn't want to let them down. I was supposed to protect all of them. It was still so very early in the morning and everyone was still asleep, except for my second oldest boy. He ran to me and buried his face in my chest, his rose and fell along with the tears that fell from his eyes.

He told me that my daughter had gone out with her friends. I was worried but I went upstairs to lie down. I just wanted to crawl inside myself. I wanted the pain to go away. I felt like I was in a horrid dream then I felt someone touching me.

I didn't want to be touched!

I forced his hands off of me and yelled for him to stop. What made him think I even wanted to be bothered? My son had just been murdered! when I felt someone touch me in a way that I didn't want to be touched, I said stop touching me, what makes you think I even want you to touch me. My Son has just been Murdered!

I was in a human wrapped inside of a zombie. After a few hours I went down stairs. Loved ones appeared everywhere. Some cleaning, some huddled in corners moping and holding each other. They all showed love to me in different ways.

However, the father of my children, the man who knew my son since he was six months old, hurt me in the midst of my tragedy. His words were cruel and unkind.

"If you can't feed or clothe the kids then get the fuck out!!" he yelled. That basically meant that my family wasn't welcome in his home. That meant that me or my emotions weren't welcomed either. I questioned him but right after I put on my sunglasses and left. I needed my mom more than ever. The week went by and I could not tell day from night. My sons side of the family helped to make the home going arrangements.

During it all, my husband decided to try and pull me away from my family as they prepared to say their goodbyes. Then, he wanted to take control of everything. He had to be in charge of the children. Arrangements had to be done and they had to be at his family's house.

My kids would come and try to pull me away at the end of my long days. Everybody wanted to know where the boy was. The one who disrespected our family and killed my son. Uncles, cousins, brothers and other loved ones patrolled the streets. They asked around and finally got a lead. They didn't find the shooter but they found someone who knew just as much.

It was a young lady who was in the bathroom when it happened. They guy everyone searched for was her boyfriend. Relief traveled through the air but it still wouldn't bring my son back to me.

We hoped his fate would be worse than death.

Everyone sat outside on the stairs outside of my sons place as she revealed what happened. Moments later the police arrived at the shooters house.

It wasn't just Albany Policeman looking for him. It was Colonie Police, US Marshals and the FBI. They wanted his grandmother too. She'd been on America's Most Wanted for drug trafficking. My sons aunt said that boy was born a demon. His question "how did you find me?" trailed off as an

omission of guilt. His arrest brought only a small comfort.

Chapter Fifteen

My sons father and my husband both accompanied me at the funeral home for arrangements. They were cordial for the first time since the fight back in 1982. I never wanted that to happen but it did. It's true what they say about death and appreciating life. It makes you forget about all the unnecessary drama and brings people together. Elleek's father lost his only child, even though he was absent most of his life. That made me know that the grief was greater for him. Although, everyone was devastated by the misfortune. Elleek touched everyone around him; those he knew and those he didn't. He had a smile that could light up any room. If you weren't smiling he had a way of bringing it out of you. His mannerisms reflected his grandparents and my own. He loved his family. His brothers and sisters were his pride and joy.

I reflected as I remember one of the many times he made me laugh. He said "Ma holla at me, throw a dolla at me, I'll do something strange for a piece of change." My lips turned up in a slight grin at the thought but the sadness overwhelmed me.

Later that night, I had to wake up and discuss the burial. We practiced Islam in our household amongst other things. The imam called from the mosque and he discussed the arrangements with my husband. They decided when and how Elleek would be buried. My son would be placed in a wooden box on the very next day. My faith flew out of the window. After all I'd gone through that was the final straw. I refused to rush my son's burial because of my husbands need for control and his religious laws. I couldn't help but blame myself. I felt that after all the praying I'd done and doing the right thing didn't come in handy. How could this happen?

"No!" I shouted.

I was done with everything. My family wanted to come and show me support to. I would not hand over one of the most important days of my life to him.

"Are you crazy? you just want to bury my son and move forward with your life!!"

He was a non-practicing Muslim but on that day he chose to bring forth all the stipulations.

He barely responded. His hesitation was further drowned out by the ringing of my phone. It was Elleeks father, he wanted his side of the family to take care of everything. I was drained and even though my son went through life without his father I gave him the okay to proceed.

I wanted a celebration of life for my son. My subconscious tried to rear about the religion but I brushed it off. Whether it was right or wrong it didn't matter because my son's life was just shortened by the young punk who decided to play God.

Why? He was a coward who was afraid to ask for a fair fight. I pushed the thoughts to the side and met up with my family.

I had them coming from all over. Some came from North Carolina, some from Georgia and other places. I felt so much love and I needed it. I gathered old and recent pictures of Elleek to put his program together. Some were colored and some were black and white. I nearly stayed up all night, restless.

Everything had to be perfect for my son. I decided to have some of the children and a few adults wear shirts with his pictures placed on the front.

The morning after, we stood outside the funeral home. I looked at the faces of those around me and thought that it seemed as if death made you famous. I had some people who loved me and wanted to support me. Then there were those who didn't care, they just wanted to see me under pressure. The final ones just wanted to see what the face of a mother who had just lost her son looked like.

I wore a blue piece of garment that covered my body and head which was the Islamic attire. My kids father and my husband were near me but I wouldn't let either one console me. My cousin was there and she held me up as we approached the door. Once inside, we walked down a squeaky but silent hallway. It seemed to take miles.

The room was cool and adorned in dim lighting. I felt empty. I felt like I had nothing left or no one. It seemed as if my life had just begun and yet I had to say goodbye to someone who meant the world to me, someone I always saw in my future. Nothing I did was good enough to allow him to stay with me just a little bit longer. The overpowering grief and tears of sorrow seemed to never end. I spotted Elleek and I couldn't take the next step....I started to breathe heavy as if I was in labor and as we walked I had to concentrate on my breathing. It felt like I was back in that room giving birth to him. Instead it was the end of his life. My Cousin held my hand, God bless her for being by my side. As we walked, those that knew my son were standing, some sitting. Emotions were flying everywhere.

I sat in the middle next to my cousin. My children were all in the row ahead of me with the rest of my family. The soloist sang mournful songs, the pastor preached, people spoke, and it all flew over me. Everyone talked about how such a young life was lost and said comforting words to myself and loved ones. I had to get up several times to hug and kiss my children who were crying and just so sad, it was the hardest thing.

It was crazy how everyone came together but were was everyone before that? He needed so much but it was over. Was I expected to pick up the pieces and move on?

My oldest children had resilience and my youngest three didn't really understand. The service was unbearable but there was so much love and I felt it, even in the midst of my pain.

The eyes of my sons father revealed so much. I could only imagine what it was like for him to lose his only son. I still had eight left. I went to him and we hugged. We embraced each other for the love we had for our chile. I know he wished that he played his role differently.

A young lady came up to me and she happened to be the mother of Elleeks unborn son. They'd lost him a little while before. She handed me the baby's book with the yurn. He wanted me to the book and put the yurn in the casket so their son could be with him.

Everyone spoke of how good he looked but once I made it closer, I noticed the blood still on his finger nails. Enraged I asked myself, How could they be so insensitive and allow me to see this? It made me think of the horrible event that lead up to the place I stood. My son was the most handsome young man to ever walk the earth. But he lay there, lifeless. His amazing zest for life ripped away. I prayed for his peace. I just didn't know how I was expected to move on. Everyone promised to do anything they could for me but nothing was satisfying because no one could bring my son back to me. Someone did that to my son, he wasn't sick, he wasn't infected with some impossible disease. No! His life was taken by some young kid who didn't value his own. My son was twenty four years old.

I sat and only thought of justice for my son. I really wanted something to be done.

My cousin wanted to speak on behalf of me and Elleek. She spoke about senseless murdering and she said a life was taken so a life could live. She knew what I was battling and what Elleek had gone through before he was killed.

She also was speaking in general because it was someone there probably going through the same thing.

I was touched by the amount of people who came out to show their love for my son. I didn't know everyone but I was still grateful because I knew they were there based on who he was an individual. It wasn't about who he ran with or who he was related to. Some call funerals a celebration of one's life. That wasn't a celebration.

It was no secret that my son was in the streets and did some things that I wouldn't approve of but he didn't deserve that.

My cousin was speaking to everyone when she said a life taken so a life could live.

The pain of losing someone you love is very real but the pain of losing a child is endless.

Preparing for the cemetery was even more tragic. I felt my legs limp underneath me as the casket was soon closed off and my son left the world. Forever.

I will never, ever forget you. Your life, your words, your pain or your fears. You were my first born whom I cherished with my heart and soul..

Life already felt different without Elleek. The ride to Graceland Cemetery was bumpy along a winding road that curved all the way down the hill. How was I going to go on without seeing his handsome face?

I was so proud to call him my son. He went back to school and got a decent job. I was so happy he listened to me. But as I watch the casket get lowered into the ground, I ask scold him one last time as a mother and ask; Why do I have to do this?

Chapter Sixteen

Two years had passed since Elleek was brutally murdered while celebrating his 24th birthday. His killer was a 17-year-old high school dropout.

The young coward was let out on bail after being arrested previously for robbery and a gun charge. I didn't understand the justice system. Why was he even let back out on the street with that type of rep sheet?

The jury selection is what concerned me the most. There were six white men, six white women and only one black person. It was obvious who would determine whether or not the boy would be found guilty. Everyone knew he fit the crime. The evidence was clear. I thought to myself that a guilty conviction wouldn't bring my son back but it would give me the respect I deserve as a mother. It would've given me some type of rest and a feeling that I could still believe in the justice system.

Court was set to start at 9 am and I got settled right in the first set of wooden benches. My kids father sat next to me. I wanted the jury to see my face and wondered if it would make a difference.

The boy came out and he looked much different than before. His previous short braids were gone and he rocked a brush cut. He didn't resemble his mug shot. The look was gone too. The one that showed his eyes opened real wide, revealing his love for being a criminal. It was the look that he had the night he fired three shots into my son's precious body, at close range. Close enough for bystanders to see him. He fumbled across the courtroom, shackled with handcuffs around his hands and ankles. He was wearing a light blue button down shirt with a pink tie. Khaki pants covered his worn buster brown shoes.

The judge went through his normal process of asking the jury various questions. The one that stuck with me the most was Is there anyone who has any type of relationship with the defendant? Of course that would be a conflict of interest. Someone that worked in the school district was asked to leave because she was an obvious connection. They continued to weed out the rest of the jury and that is how they came up with their final number.

We were told to go home and to return the next day. There was a woman who would testify. She was approached by Elleeks killer and asked if she could buy him some bullets. I was all ready for everything to be over. The feeling in my gut said I couldn't go on because there would be unbearable things that I wouldn't want to witness but I had no choice. I ignored the twist in my stomach and prepared for another day at court.

We adjourned the same time on the following day. I prepped my attire and made a light breakfast. I didn't want to get dizzy or have a headache from the lack of nutrition. I needed my energy to ensure I would make it through the duration of sitting.

The testifier stated that she knew the defendant. He and her son played together as a boy. So when he ran into her at the store, he decided to ask her to buy the bullets. That proved it was premeditated murder. However, she refused to help him and never saw him after that. It was enough to prove that he was the shooter and the one who had intentions on killing my son.

Their next witness was my sons uncle. The little punk didn't know his environment or the graphics of where he lived because he approached my sons uncle. It was a hot summer day and he did his next bidding outside of a small store in the neighborhood. He asked him for if he had an ID and then tried his chances again by asking him to purchase bullets. Uncle turned him down and let him know he wouldn't do it.

The district attorneys made their case next. They pointed out that the murder was plotted and planned. They said the young boy knew he would kill my son before his event. The next witness was a young lady who was at the party that night. She talked about how my son was so ready to celebrate his birthday. I'll never forget her face or her words. She had so much pain and distress in her testimony and it put me right where I didn't want to be. It made me think of my own sons pain. Damn! I thought to myself and prayed a recess was coming soon. I really needed a breath of fresh air to process everything.

We got one shortly after her testimony was over and I sent one up above. Out in the hallway, family from both sides gathered. It was loud and hectic. My side silently blamed theirs for not raising their son right. They were responsible too. Maybe if they taught him the value of life things would have turned out differently. He obviously didn't value his own.

We returned back to the courtroom and I started to notice all of the people around me. Heads were turning and people were whispering everywhere. I tried to keep my eyes focused and in front of me. My eyes wanted to stay on the person who took my son from me. His face will forever be implanted in my mind.

I wasn't feeling good with all the cross examination. I felt like I would go into cardiac arrest at any moment. The district attorney called up the "person of interest" and his yellow jumpsuit lit up the courtroom. I never really knew what one looked like until that day. He was brought down from Albany County Jail. I watched him as the next witness took the rom.

It was a young man, big and black. He was the killer's accomplice. He said he didn't see anything and that he only drove my son to the hospital to get help in the backseat of her car. On his way to the hospital he looked in the backseat and saw that Elleek was already gone.

The wrenching testimony from his mouth put me in a silence of disbelief. I looked around the courtroom and knew he was protecting him. Hhe definitely had more to hide.

He was probably paid off; his job complete while my sons case seemed to be falling by the waist side.

The final day of court arrived. I was sitting alone and everything was bleak. I was anxious to know what would come next. My heart was heavy but I tried to remain optimistic. I was prepared for whichever outcome it would be. Nothing would bring my son back. On the other end, I wanted to trust in God and hoped that justice would prevail.

The verdict was received. I noticed that the courtroom was more packed than it was during the trial. My heartbeat was pounding faster and harder than ever before.

The judge entered the court and everyone stood to their feet. Once he sat down he turned to the jury and asked the awaited question "Has the jury reached a verdict?

A note was sent to the judge to explain the definition of reasonable doubt. I thought to myself, how? and why? There was no reason for any doubt.

I looked for the jury as they walked back in after more discussion. I wanted to get a sense of what they might have been thinking. I couldn't seem to tell so I just said a small prayer to myself.

The judge asked the question again and this time they had a final verdict. "Yes, we have your honor" The response rang in my ear. "All rise" says the judge.

I could hear the beats of my heart in my ear drums. The jury reads " We the jury find the defendant Not Guilty of Murder....... on all counts."

The screams of the defendants family screaming "Yes" were lost in the devastation of mine. My teary eyed family stormed out of the building in defeat. If was as if we found out for the first time that Elleek was murdered. I held in how I was feeling and for the longest I just stood there, immobile. I watched the boy who killed my son, my first born child and saw the relief and joy on his face from being found innocent. He had the look of someone who had just gotten away with cold blooded murder. My heart broke for my other children and I had to console them while the other family laughed and rejoiced.

That day ended and after that our lives were through to the press. they had been following the story since the day of Elleeks death. I also spoke out about how gun violence affected my family and the community. Everyone wanted to hear what I had to say. They wanted to know my pain and my feelings after what happened.

I told them the only thing I could and that was God had a plan and my family had to move forward. I just hated my family had to relive everything over and over again.

"What kind of system do we have? What kind of laws don't protect the innocent? What kind of message are we sending our youth?"

We were headed home after my speech and as we were stopped at the traffic light, a man jumped out of the car in front of us. He started punching another person seeming to have the upper hand but soon after pulls out a sharp object and starts stabbing his victim with it. I couldn't believe my eyes. I looked over at the driver and his body jerked. The guys hand pierced his stomach over and over. I looked back out of the window in shock. I had never before saw anything as deadly up close and personal. The wound was still so fresh from my own sons murder and I wondered why that would happen so soon after his verdict. I took it as a sign. A sign that violence is so widespread that we often turn a blind eye to it. Where does it end?

The rest of the day was empty, final and lonely. The fight was over of convincing and trying to take a stance. Our city was divided, some upset and some happy.

Chapter Seventeen

Letter to the jury...

As Jury Member I'm sure you're not new to the Gun Violence that is at an all-time High in the City of Albany and surrounding Cities. If you are a Mother or Father then you know where I'm coming from if you don't then you have no form of reference...However even though you are giving instructions on what to do and what not to do during the trial before you came into being a juror you had to have some common sense. However, I have my reservations on how the pick was with only one black, the rest white, might as well say an all-white jury that one black voice didn't even matter. On March 10, 2008 you acquitted the person that gunned down my son and brutally murdered him. How did you feel about that?, Did you say, we don't care one less Nigga we have to worry about robbing us or violating any of us? We could care less if they want to keep killing each other? Did you say in your mind, well one is gone, if we lock up the one being charged then he won't be able to kill anymore and it's in our best interest if they do it for us? It wasn't no big deal we knew he was out on bail for an attempted robbery, so he wasn't robbing us so we don't care? We also knew it was gang related and we know what gang members do, although the judge wouldn't allow any materials in the court of The Gang nature that right there should have given you a lot to think about. The fact that it was the prosecutor word against the defense attorneys because of bad communication didn't have nothing to do with the fact that my son was killed in cold blood, the driver put him in her car, with the Gun in his hand how is that not valid?! Did you hear that? Not to mention, of this prior the boy who murdered my son was shot and there was testimony given that him and the other boy shot had gang affiliation, yet nothing Gang related was allowed in the courtroom. That case was brought up in the case, were you not paying attention? Again, if the boy who was murdered or if my son had been white the outcome would have been different, those are the facts no lies! Gang members move and do things in a way that the judge wouldn't let be explained, but as a jury you were supposed to see right through that. All you did was obvious, let a Cold blooded killer go on a ramp page. Committing Crime until you're a victim you'll never know. Once this Murderer was free he was boasting and bragging by getting a tattoo that reads "not guiltily" and another one that reads "Gangstas never snitch". If you didn't know, now you know, that you didn't do anything good and up standing as he remained free he even faced a new robbery charge, and was in a large scale federal case, which falls under the rico statute gang related selling drugs having guns conspiracy the whole 9. At the age of 23 he admitted to being an intruder who wore masks and tied up victims in October 2009...how does that make you feel jury? I pray no one else's fate is in your hands. What does integrity mean to you? What does the word justice mean to you? Strong moral principles, fairness also, honesty, the state of being whole and undivided. Justice, peace, and genuine respect for people. How did you appeal to giving justice to my Son? You didn't think about him at all. The fact the at the age of 24 years old you too help take his life by not giving the Murderer his just due. It wasn't about just sitting there and listening, the evidence and track record of this boy that you found guilty on all counts!!! Yet he walked free to commit more crimes and mayhem. Had the decision been Guilty has charged, things would have been different. I'm sure it wouldn't have made the pain any easier to deal with because my son was Murdered in cold blood. It may have allowed closure to happen at a different rate, I don't know. What I do know is that seeing the boy who Murdered your loved one walk and play and live and breathe is the hardest thing ever to have to face. It's about holding you and officials accountable, apparently judges can't be held accountable. Indictment dismissed, charges dropped on a technicality, pertinent evidence and information not admissible and allowed in the courtroom. It's obvious to a duck that this was a hung jury. I hope this at least gives everyone a conscious, in the event that you ever have to decide what someone's fate will be or how you play a part in that. You may feel that I am wrong in my observation or your nothing like what I described. I can't blame everyone for the crime that one person did however if you played a part in the situation at all I'm sorry, it was my Son and that's how I feel. Nothing, will change that, you had time to sit amongst each other and brainstorm to decide whether or not this boy actually killed my Son. Ultimate time did tell he did kill my Son and got away with it. If you keep up with the News you see that he was set free but still committing crimes still being a violator still being a menace to society. All that is done he on Earth, where people have freedom of choice to say and do as they please. However as long as it doesn't infringe on anyone else's rights. No jury or No judge could ever give the punishment that is the one he will receive for Murdering my Son. Every move he makes my Son is turning over in his Grave waiting for justice to be done.

Chapter Eighteen

It was an awful thing to have happened to my loved ones. To have someone so close to us murdered with his killer set free was more than too much for us to bare. I didn't know how I would ever heal from it.

I guess it's true that whatever doesn't kill you makes you stronger. I also had the love and support from my family and friends. They were always there when I needed them. I will never forget my son running up to me saying "Ma".

I soon felt strong enough to speak to the media more about how I felt. I took them back to the same spot where my son was gunned down. 343 Sheridan Ave is where my son was shot 4 times. I'm never going to forget that night. Neither will the rest of the City. My Family was in a very disturbed state of mind right , I wasn't the only one affected.

I started to become very angry and I feel I had every right to be. The boy who killed my son was living free with breath in his body. It meant he was free to commit another murder. I wondered if I should feel threatened as well. Please don't tell me how to feel.

I just knew I had to put everything in God's hand and let him decide the outcome. I didn't know if it was death or jail but I knew that young man was headed for self-destruction. I found it hard to now want him to suffer like my son. However, I knew that as humans we cannot give or take live. Besides, nothing I or anyone else did could do what my Lord would have in store. Even the judge couldn't be held accountable.

I saw his parents around and wondered why they thought it was okay. Other people also encountered him and would tell me how he walked around like he was invincible. I didn't really understand why they told me unless it was to warn me. They were probably just as amazed as I was. I mean I understood double jeopardy but seriously What the fuck?

Who did he think he was? You kill someone and then do a little time to be back walking the streets. Where were the real vigilantes? Because he wasn't one. He was a coward ass punk and someone who couldn't stand to go to to to and stand up like a man.

The entire system needed to be changed. It would've changed my life and the lives of everyone who loved my son. The girl who lied on the stand was probably the main reason my sons killer walked free. It was her testimony. I knew her family so I trusted her story at first. Maybe I had mixed emotions. I knew that her story was fabricated to appease the court and district attorney. I ran into her a couple places after that and in my head I said You Selfish Bitch!!

She was thinking more about her life and that's why she didn't go to the police immediately. She was scared she was next but it only gave the coward time to prepare. Things went the way they did because she covered for him.

I was driving one day and he passed me. I only knew it was him because he started to drive slow for a while. He stared right in my face. Unbelievable!

If looks could kill, I would've died right on the spot. He was driving an all-white BMW. I was so upset when I saw him. I told my boyfriend and he told me not to worry that the young coward would have to deal with what he did someday. I felt powerless.

I spotted him again another day on my lunch break. At first glimpse I wasn't sure but I decided to get out of my car anyway. Then, I thought I should get back in my car and leave but why did I have to do that?

It just made me fear for my life and I thought I needed to stay armed too. However, I went in the store in the midst of my uncertainty. On the inside he was laughing of a crowd who was doing the same. I stood close enough to see the tattoo everyone spoke about. It read clearly "Not Guilty". As I stood there waiting my turn I felt like I was failing my son by standing so close to his murderer without doing anything.

Once he felt me staring at him, he looked, burst out laughing and ran outside. I finally got my order and left feeling like I let Elleek down.

I wish I had done something because he later tried to get with one of my younger daughters. They were out and about when he approached her. That was a low blow. It was very malicious.

On another occasion my oldest daughter was out with some friends. They were at a bar and Elleeks killer was there in circle of some people she considered family. She was ready to crack his skull!

She screamed at him "how is it okay for you to be on trial for murdering my brother and still live as if you did nothing?!!" As she went in preparation of throwing the bottle someone pulled her back. they told her to let it go. I held her later that night in my bed and comforted her.

Then I cried because we found out that we were related to him. I didn't know how to move forward.

Chapter Nineteen

Elleek's birthday was May 15, on May 16th he lost his life, on May 19th we mourned and on the 20th we said goodbye. As I wrote on my paper and recalled the events that took place one person came to mind. It was the big black boy who befriended my son and then took his life after he only lived to be 24 years old for 30 minutes. He plotted and planned to kill my son and his mission was accomplished. What a terrible thing he did but I knew one day he would be held accountable.

It was a Saturday morning. I had stayed in bed really late weeks after the trial was over. Every day I woke up looking for a reason to live. I realized that I had to keep going ahead because I still had eight children to see about and I loved them dearly. Their lives had to be enough for me to go on.

However, I still wanted to see justice done. All I wanted was for the people responsible to pay in this life, I knew they would pay in the next. I laid in my bed staring out the window asking God why?

The next morning my kids were up and running around. I refused to get out of bed to deal with them but the phone rang. After my son, I became an emotional nervous wreck anytime I heard it buzz, especially early in the morning. It startled me but I got up to answer it. The person on the other end addressed me by an old nickname. Haneefa.

"Who is this?" I asked

"It's me" they replied

I repeated the question because I still wasn't sure who it was and thought it was some sort of prank. I finally realized who it was and asked what was up.

"He's dead" I heard her say.

"What do you mean he's dead?" I thought for sure it was Elleek's killer.

My heart pounded and my mind went into a state or disbelief. I sat up in my bed and grabbed my chest. I asked if she was sure and she confirmed she was. My first thought was that one of my loved ones did something and that made me fearful. But she told me that the young boy who lied on the stand had died in a car crash. She was at the hospital because she was sick and they brought him in.

It believed it has an act of God! All praises went to the Creator who is the giver and taker as life. As far as I was concerned he finally paid for his crime. He lied and my son's killer went free while we suffered.

He had gone to the club to rob several people of their jewelry and afterwards took the cops on a high-speed chase. Later he was found wrapped around a tree. His brother was in the car with him but it wasn't his time. They said when the car hit the tree, the impact killed him immediately.

Although, I never wanted to wish death on anyone else's child I felt like my prayers from that morning were answered. I just wanted some form of justice.

I had lost hope but at that moment I felt as if a huge weight was lifted off of my shoulders. I then had the energy to get up to make breakfast for my family. Respectfully, as a mother, I still felt bad for his because when things like that happens nobody really wins. In the end all was lost and ended in his own self-destruction. They say an eye for an eye but at the end of the day we're all left blind. But karma is a bitch!

My lost faith in God was restored that morning and somehow all my years of prayers were answered. Even though his mother had to lose her son too, justice was served for the crime committed against my son. Before his death he laid low feeling invincible. In the end he knew he wasn't in control. He felt the wrath of God. Everybody has their own definition of what karma is. However, understand that if you do something to someone else the same may not happen to you but you will somehow suffer and feel the pain you caused others.

Chapter Twenty

How do we rise and stand before we fall and become victims of black on black crime? Why as a family, a community or as a nation do we allow self-destruction to be a part of our makeup? When will we break the chains of silence and do something to prevent this corruption and violence? And it can happen to you… or a loved one.

Soon after my son was murdered I became bitter, angry, and wanted something done about what happened. I made connections with politicians, clergymen, the media, and anyone in the community that supported change of any kind. I was without a doubt, not going to let my emotions lye doormat inside. I went back to my roots. I was born from a mother who came into the world in 1917 and my father not far from behind her. They came up North during a time where African Americans were first earning their rights. I felt blessed and grateful for having them as parents. It taught me how to speak out against injustice especially after my son was murdered. I had never in my life felt so much pain.

So when the Media wanted to do an interview I couldn't wait. It wasn't something I had to think about at all. The pain came out in my words but they wanted to hear my voice so I gave it to them. On many other occasions someone tried to silence me, but this was the time for me to be silenced no more. Once I did the first interview, all of the News Stations wanted to hear my feelings and wanted to see my emotions. I held hard onto my tears but they came out.

Then community leaders wanted to give their condolences, and wanted to invite me to speak out at local events. Soon I met with politicians regarding what happened to my son, and what could they do about it. I attended community meetings in City Hall where many concerned citizens spoke out about the issues in the community and how it affected them and their families. I signed in on the list basically to speak about what happened to my son and how preventative measures needed to be taken to prevent the same outcome in the future. I was encouraged by most of everyone around me. There was a another lady who they called to speak. She was the nurse on the night President Reagan was shot and brought into the ER. She actually live right near me and spoke about the same issues surrounding gun violence. She was the chapter leader for NYAGV. After the meeting was over she came and introduced herself to me. She thought since we are advocating for the same thing we should co-leaders for the organization. I was very much interested so we exchanged phone numbers and arranged to meet to get started right away, I thought to myself that it was an excellent way to get my voice heard. With gun violence being an all-time high, we organized and set up literature about gun safety focusing on sensible gun laws.

We later became a part of the wall in the lobby. From there healing began with me using my voice. The lady and I became close friends and she helped me get through it all. She realized my passion for writing, and referred me to a writing class that she once took. Writing opened up my heart and allowed my mind to be free of the pain and sorrow I felt every day. I met remarkable people that encouraged and supported me. They shared their stories as well.

Shortly after that my dear friend and my co leader were asked to do an interview, we did. My son was the angel that walked with me and guided my steps every time I mentioned his name.

I was nominated to be on a committee led by the common counsel. They were encouraged by one of my previous speeches. The committee was called the Albany Gun Violence Task Force, of which 7 was appointed by the common counsel and 6 appointed by the Mayor's office. I represented the mothers and families who lost their children to the streets and gun violence. I was the voice for those who couldn't find theirs. But I couldn't do it alone. I wanted something profound in my sons name. For the first two years we had a candlelight vigil in the vacant lot where the boy hid before killing my son. The community pitched in to make it beautiful and I was grateful. I felt as if I was just beginning to live my life.

Chapter Twenty-One

Dear El-leek,

Today is Saturday May 26, 2018 and the weather is Hot! Just how you would like it. It is your birthday month, your birthday just passed. Wow! 36 years old you would have been. We celebrated for you, your Sister Tahirah, big head, as you would always call her, made it all happened. She's always asking what we will do for you each year. So you know of course we're going to do something because you wouldn't have it any other way. You always celebrated with your friends and family. I'm at work right now and I have a little downtime. I'm always keeping busying. Nothing much has changed but I am actually a CNA now. Before you left me I was in training to be one but I hadn't finished. I had to take some time off to make sure you were situated. But I wanted to complete the course so I'm now certified. I wish you were here celebrating with us. It was a little different this year. I guess because we had a natural place outside of the location where you were murdered. I'm sorry to recall those events ,it's not something I want to hear.

Your sister went out to get t-shirts made with your picture on it. She also got a big poster with us at church. It had four different poses on it. It was beautiful. You have two little nephews right now. One is going to be a year and one is six. One is by your baby sister, believe it or not. Your oldest sister just graduated from Bryant and Stratton. Remember that is the school you were going to. We all went there but your brother didn't finish. He is doing well though. He has two jobs now and your little brother is a police officer and marine. You would be so proud of him right now.

I hate to say this but your baby brother ran into some trouble, something just like the stuff that you had to go against. I know if you were here you'd do something about it. You would be protecting your younger brothers. One of them is gone. He has custody of one of your other brothers because he couldn't chance losing another sibling. He misses you dearly. But your sister she's doing well. She was married to her son's father. She is stronger than I was. She is not accepting anything less that she deserves. She had a little setback but she pulled herself right back up and graduated from cosmetology school. She's also working on becoming a personal trainer and she stays healthy. You would be so proud of her.

And of course big head moved back home with me. She was always so close to grandma. You know that. You had ups and downs but she's back home. She is working on becoming self-sufficient. I left out the main thing. I am finally out of that bad situation. I left the situation shortly after you left me. I held on for all the wrong reasons. I try not to live in regret but it is hard sometimes because I know how those that could've made things different. Life hasn't been easy but it has gotten better. I had learned to depend on my and take care of myself.

Your baby sister isn't a baby anymore. She is about to be 15. Where did the time go? The last time you seen her you was telling her to get out of the refrigerator. It was Mother's Day. Still hurts that you're not here. There are so many things we haven't done yet. I just continue to hold onto the good memories. I look at our pictures to remember you. That is the easy part. The hardest part is not being hold you and kiss you.

I'm glad everybody's doing all right everybody loves you so much. Your siblings always as if I'm okay. I'm striving to be every day. I am not exactly where I want to be but I am so glad I'm not where I used to be.

It's Ramadan and I am not practicing like I did back then but I have the opportunity to teach myself all over. I love you so much. I am trying to live in the moment because I know that tomorrow is not promised. You really did change my life. I am writing a book called "Full circle of life was taken So a Life could live". I'm Telling our story, But it's my journey now Son. I love you miss so much I carry you with me all the time. Love Always #1 Son Mommy ❤1

Chapter Twenty-Two

I decided that I wanted to create a community garden in the area where my son was killed. I wanted to make something special after it was trashed before by the same team of people. I thought I could create a memorial garden where people could stop by to smell the flowers and just sit down to have some positive moments. I was determined to turn the negative into something good. I started taking it upon myself to clean up the lot. It was owned by someone but apparently they were not caring for it. So, I organized the community cleanup. Everyone pitched in a great deal. Year after year I would have a candlelight with a memorial picnic on my son's birthday. People came in their cars to gather around just to show their love and support. Eventually I was told that I was doing too much on someone else's property. I tried to look into the owners and the city didn't have the records. It ended up going on sale and the property was purchased for me. I was truly grateful.

There were two schools located on the block. I reached out to both schools and asked for their support in helping me to create a community memorial garden. They loved the idea of it.

Once I received the not guilty verdict everything seemed to spiral out control. I was so lost emotionally. My mom passed away along with her pride and joy which was my son.

I took a little hiatus and once I returned the property was no longer mine. It had been sold by my ex-husband.

During my journey of healing there were times when I felt very empowered. I had so much support but I still returned back to what you would call a dysfunctional situation. I was at the mercy of a person who did not care about my healing process. But God looked out for me.

There was a lot in the south where my son grew up and the pretty much offered it to me as long as I promised to take care of it. I looked to the support I had from the community and got back on my journey. I was still able to dedicated the spot in memory of my son and all of those who lost their lives to gun violence.

The Mayor of the Fire Chief and Nonprofit Organizations came out along with other community leaders to support the Garden. and other community leaders came out in supported this Garden. It was not only going to be in memory of the victims but it would also allow people in the community to have access to fresh fruits and vegetables. They could participate and benefit as well. There was also a documentary done, by a few youth in the community. They named if "Seeds of Hope."

I was able to appeal to so many people. I was not only a voice for mothers but I was able to appeal to the youth who needed someone to help guide them and offer them hope. I wanted to possibly prevent them from going down the wrong road.

I had two lots that were vacant and in much need of revitalization. Creating the vision and helping gun violence in the community was very much needed. It was especially needed in the smaller cities because the awareness could be made very easily.

It was time to start holding our elected officials accountable. There were so many vacant lots and abandoned buildings. There still is. When you wake up and see your city and your hometown you can see it is a sad situation. You probably feel as if no real progress is being made. Why should you?

Not much has changed today. There is still a lot of the same destruction going on. Drugs and violence continues to be at an all time high.

There should be better opportunities created and training focused on helping the youth change their conditions. The murders seemed to be overlooked. No real justice is hardly served. The Mayhem police force do not feel like they are paid enough to go the extra mile. They refuse to put their necks on the line. They don't really even value their positions.

Currently the lot where I did my garden is vacant. The sign is sitting in my house because of someone's selfish ways. People need to start creating change. Our schools aren't even safe anymore but I think it goes beyond Gang Violence. It is also a mental health issue...

Chapter Twenty-Three

A reflection of the present and the past

My son and so many others suffer from mental illnesses. Some may find that as a shock. However, people close to him knew that he had a temper, they just didn't know why. The illness goes undetected because we don't want the labels and the work that comes along with it. But it lies around us in every corner. It is dangerous. It ruins the lives of our children causing our families to suffer. There are far too many deaths. The signs are there in the beginning.

It all starts at home. Domestic violence is very strong. Even emotional abuse. I suffered from through both. I may not have had blackened eyes and busted lips but the control over me was beyond repair. It affects the present. I still pushed forward but I know it my children got the tail end of it.

The signs from Elleek started to show up in school. He had issues focusing and started to act out. Possibly for attention. I am sure he had so many thoughts about what he witnessed growing up. They stayed with him and played a part in his learning abilities.

Before I even had children I, myself didn't finish school. I don't think I had any real form of references either when it came to raising them once I did give birth. Nothing came with instructions. It was even worse for me because I was an only child.

So, Elleek started to fall behind and his behavior was a way to redirect the fact that the work became difficult for him. I was at the school all the time to ensure that he was getting the most of what the school system had to offer him. Again, his behavior always became the main source of his problem. Until they put a label on him as being disabled in math. It didn't help the situation meeting with the Special Education Committees. I was the only one who attended the meetings and still had to take care of my small children as well. My Point of saying that mental health is an issue, is because when he couldn't cope with what was going on, he became frustrated. He turned to drugs and it didn't get better for him. The world spun out of control for him. It was to the point where everything that once mattered no longer did. I felt his pain because that is what mothers do. We take on the worries of our children. I just continued to try and make it better for him but it was a battle.

The situation at home didn't make it any better. He was the big brother and deep down he wanted his siblings to be proud of him, no matter what. He would put forth the effort at times but always came up short so after that he felt like an outcast. Instead of him being able to mingle with his family and feel loved by the father figure, he had to call him uncle. I think that alone drove him to dark places.

One summer at a picnic he said something to his siblings uncle that he didn't like and it got Elleek a slap in the face. It was so wrong. He tried to defend himself but no one did anything. My ex-husband beat him as well. It was called discipline but what is discipline with no love?

So he carried this to school with him and that didn't make for good learning environment. When he hit Middle School it really spiraled out of control. I knew he carried a lot of hurt and resentment in him. His anger reached a point where he no longer wanted to go to school and he started to give the staff problems. Those were all signs of a mental illness. I feel like he didn't get enough support. We never do.

I changed his school and did everything else I could think of but the end result would always be the same.

The fact that my son thought that he would be safer if he carried a gun scared the hell out of me. The streets were loaded with so many young men who were going through the same things as him. They were all lost young men who had no real male figure to teach them how to conduct themselves. He cried out many times to me that he wish he was never born and almost always felt rejected by his own father. It made him feel incomplete. I worried about him and was afraid that he would one day he would do something to himself or someone else. However, when he was happy and life was going in his favor, he showed a different side. He knew how to express times of joy and times of sadness. He also knew how to express times of frustration. He was frustrated a lot with me and some of the decisions I had to make. The fact that living life was very limited with the amount of friends that he lost to Gun Violence was creating and contributing more to his mental illness. The trauma that he was suffering by attending those funerals and seeing the shootings never left his thoughts. He always felt like he was next and that anything of a positive nature couldn't exist in his world. Imagine waking up every day having to look over your shoulder with the thought of being murdered and left for dead.

It is no life for our kids to live. But they live it every day. It didn't start with my son and it won't end with him. I just hope that somewhere and somehow the help will be given to our young men. My son wanted so much for me and I knew he wanted more for himself. I would do anything to have him back with me but God had a different plan, for the both of us.

Chapter Twenty-Four

Gang Rivalries and The Reasons behind them

There have been gangs around for as long as I can remember. Yet, back in 2006 when my son was killed it was reported that we didn't have any. We supposedly just had a loosely affiliated group of kids. There has always been issues between Troy and Albany, and Albany and Schenectady. Uptown and downtown are always in competition even with the girls. The question is why? In this small town we all know each other or our parents know each other. It's to the point where some kids grew up together and at some point even slept in the same bed. It's a terrible thing, and if you're not careful probably even related. Our young people are looking for a shoulder to cry on. They are searching for a sense of belonging and guidance. It starts with the breakdown of the family. When things go wrong at home they use that as a way to run into the streets to find people who will listen to and agree with them. It's not to say that the issues at home are not real or not that bad, they just are not getting dealt with. You may have so much abuse going on and there's so much pain that it's hard for the child to handle it. So, it starts at home with how the parents are parenting and how much support they get there, whether they are being raised by a single mother who is weak or one who is strong. There is also that two parent household which may have a different meaning. If there is no love and no true direction then the child may feel abandonment even with two parents. So they run into the streets to find the person they can relate to. That's where the slogan " it starts at home" comes from. Why do our kids do the things they do? Our kids can be angry for a lot of reasons. It could be from the lack of resources out to help them and it puts them at a lost. When we don't address the small issues they turn into big issues. The sad thing is once our children get exposed to the violence, once they shoot a few people or get shot it's no problem to go through that again. This is why we have so many murders. What is the reason we won't acknowledge that we have Gangs in our City? Because it's not rocket science.

In one part of town if someone gets shot there will be retaliation from the other part of town. Every City has Gangs some more dangerous than others but they do exist. We lack so much that our children need and so therefore our children are angry and frustrated with how they are supposed to live. They turn to selling drugs and everything else that comes with being caught up. Then when that fails they end up in jail or in the grave. Alternatively, we are left with the trauma that comes with the aftermath of it all. The parents are left without their children or vice versa and the vicious cycle continues. Time passes and our children get older but now the problem is bigger. How do we break the Cycle of Violence and stop the rivalries?

Makeshift Memorials don't really help us to heal. They just keep us in the present state of mind. They serve as a reminder of what happened in the first place so we need less of those. We need more healing and prevention. We need more solutions to aid the families that are suffering and teach them how to cope with the losses. It's not something we want to get use to but we have to know how to take care of ourselves the proper way but we still haven't. So the cycle starts again. Over and over.

ABOUT THE AUTHOR

Allison D. Williams, known as Denise, was Born in Cape, May New Jersey. At two weeks old, she was adopted and taken to Upstate New York. She currently resides in Albany County and is the Mother of 9 children. Allison has always had a passion for helping others and mostly worked in the Healthcare field. Her life was turned upside down when her first born son was brutally gunned down, while celebrating his 24th Birthday. The incident devastated and changed her life immensely.

Her book *"Full Circle: A life taken so a life could live"* is based on the tragic shooting. Allison hopes to help other Mothers heal after losing a child to violence. All proceeds from the book will go to a foundation in her son's name, Elleek T. Williams Brace. Elleek worked with young boys in the community and the foundation will continue his legacy. Since that day, Allison has dedicated herself to improving her life and the people around her. This devastating loss, along with a test of her faith caused Allison to reach a breaking point. She found her voice again by attending several events that gave back to the community.

In 2007, she joined *New Yorkers Against Gun Violence* and became Capital District Chapter Leader. Shortly after, she was nominated for the "Spirit of Justice, Unsung Hero Award". Allison applied and was selected to be a member of *Albany's Gun Violence Task Force*, along with the Chief of Police, various clergymen, council members and other dignitaries. She started using writing as another outlet and completed several writing classes at the *Art Center of the Capital District in Troy*. She will continue using her voice to stand up against violence and help communities move past tragedies.

Made in the USA
Middletown, DE
17 January 2020